To My ~~~~~
Tulani, Thank for your
prayers, and words of
encouragement. Stay
in Touch. Love you
much.
Sister Christine
Dyer.

Love Is A Journey...Short Stories of Love

Christine R. Dyer

Acknowledgement

The Author: Evangelist Christine R. Dyer would like to take you on a spiritual journey that will touch the heart of all those who read this book.

It's a journey that all of us have taken or will take in our lives. A journey that will strengthen your faith. A journey that will emotionally set you on the edge, and send you down memory lane.

"Love is a journey", is a book of short stories, about people and events,the author has encountered on her path through life. Join her as she shares touching moments,as she travels back to past heartaches and accomplishments of family and friends and see how Jesus was there in every step.

Introduction

From the Author: Christine R Dyer

This book is to encourage, uplift and stir up those vivid memories that were shared; it's about families of loved ones who have past from life to eternity. It's about maturing, faith in God and standing on the truth. Know that God can make a difference in your life and others as well.

We have all experienced love in many ways, but God's love is everlasting, until we past from life to eternity. Until we experience his love we won't know what magnitude of what real love is real, the love that you'll lay your life down for. He did that on calvary because of love. Love truly is a journey, because you grow as you go on the journey. If you would allow the growth process to take place in your life; Stop and smell the roses.

God Bless you on your Journey!

Dedication

I dedicate this book to the loving memories of my Grandparents, Aunts, and Sister who have past from life to eternity, and have impacted my life for a life-time.

Grandparents:
George and Lula D Cowan
Calvin and Pearlie M Dunklin

My Aunts:
Lillie B Dunklin
Carrie B Dunklin
Georgia Purdue
Laura Zene

Sister:
Shirlene Renee Reeves

My mom, A Woman of Prayer

I watched my mom pray often; as long as I
could remember, I never heard her use foul
language. However, I did see her angry, but
even in her anger she had integrity. She had a
favorite word she used. Her word was "Jesus."
She has a way of saying Jesus. You will know if
you did something wrong or if she was pleased
with you, the way she said Jesus. My mom was
introduced to Christ by my father. She would
often say she didn't need saving, my father
did. She felt she was basically a good person.
Although she was a good person, she realized
she needed God in her life.

On one occasion my brother Steve had taken
ill when he was a baby. He was near death.
This was a time when she had to make a
conscious decision. My brother was in
intensive care. At the time my mom was the
only one allowed in the hospital room with my
brother. I believed this is just how God
planned it. She said she began to cry out to
God if he saved her baby from death, she will

give her life to him. Well, God spared my brother Steve's life. My mom kept her promise to God.

During the years raising us, she faced many obstacles. We live on the north side of Chicago. The north side of Chicago was gang infested in the 1960's. Mom and dad had five boys and three girls, we were not exempt from gangs. We were approached to join different gangs several times. My mother use to get down beside our beds and pray for us. She would ask God to go with us and protect us. God did protect us.

Other families where we lived had to send their children south to live with other relatives. There were eight of us they could not send all of us away, prayer worked. In those days if you didn't join a gang you would be found some where you didn't want to be. On one occasion, my oldest brother Sam was approached several times, he told my mother about being approached. She went to the throne of prayer, we could hear her pray. This prayer was a little more intense than usual, as she interceded on our behalf.

My brother was taken by the gang to a place called cloud nine on the roof top of a building, they beat him, but didn't kill him. They told him if he didn't join the gang he would be thrown from the roof top. He said he told the gang members his mom was a praying woman of God. He also told them that he couldn't join for fear that his mom would tell the Lord what he had done somehow. Sam knew that my mother was praying and God would work a miracle for him. I believe prayer caused the gang to release Sam. We believed in our mother's prayers and the gang never bothered him again.

During those trying years God kept us safe. We faced many things young people go through such as: peer pressure and wanting to do the same things other children were doing. Our parents were strict, or so we thought at the time. We were taught in a Christian home to do what was right, although we didn't always do it. At the time I use to say I hate my parents for the way they were. But down

the road of life, I thank God for the
discipline.

As time past we moved to the south side of
Chicago a better atmosphere. Our parents
still had the same rules. As we grew older I
could see changes in my father, he decided to
do things differently, he completely stop
going to church. Our family was changing we
were not going places together anymore. My
mom was truly a woman of prayer. I couldn't
understand her composure, when my father
was getting ready to go out, she wouldn't say
anything about the changes he was making at
least not in front of my siblings or I. She still
cooked his food and washed his clothes. She
made sure she was the perfect wife to my
father.

However, I didn't see it that way. I would say
little things like "he would cook his own food if
it was me". Did I know what I was saying? I
got into a disagreement with my mother. I
told her I didn't want to be like her, and if
this is what living for the Lord is about, then
I couldn't do it. At the time I couldn't see my

mom as being a strong woman, I told her with my bad attitude, when I grow up I was going to be my own woman. I am going to do as I please. I was young at the time I didn't understand what she must be feeling. I was angry, because I felt our father was being taken slowly away from us by the things of the world.

My father did a lot of things for my mother. He bought her clothes, he picked out the furniture, he cooked, and cleaned. I thought this was his choice, but mom liked the way my father did things and she didn't seem to mind. They were always together but things had changed with our family. I'm sure this was a painful adjustment to my mom. However, she rose to the occasion because she had a relationship with God. She was happy in the Lord, she had that inner joy. I now know what that scripture mean "the joy of the Lord is my strength", He surely was hers.

As I grew and matured I began to see my mother in a different light. I saw God transforming her. She wasn't just a mother,

God had instilled some deep things inside of
her and she had to release them. I'm sure if
she could tell the story, she would tell you
how shy she was. She couldn't talk to anyone
but my father. She allowed the Lord to mold
and make her. I thought when my father
passed away, she would go back into her shell,
but on the contrary she blossomed. She faced
many trials and tribulations in her life.

The death of my oldest brother Sam, was
devastating, he was taken from us abruptly.
He was killed from a gun shot wound and died
on the way to the hospital. Sam had won a
four year scholarship to college, but never
had the chance to go. It was such a tragedy,
an isolated incident. We still don't know the
details as to what really happened. We all
believed Sam to have been my mom's favorite
child, even though she would deny it, she said
she loved all of her children the same. Sam
was different he had his own way of doing
things. My mom always said Sam loved her,
because he showed it.

During the trying times of her life I saw her

shed many tears but fall on her face and looked to God for strength. He gave it to her. I don't know what it was like for her to loose a son, but I do know what it was like for me to lose a brother.

My mom lost many people in her life, her sister Georgia to breast cancer. Auntie Georgia was like one of my mom's children. Her mom and dad, auntie Laura, uncle Henry and her daughter, Shirlene. It was such a shock to everyone, that my sister Shirlene died in her sleep, she suffered from diabetes and it's complications, for many years.

Mom grieved, but again God was her source of strength. Although there were trials, it didn't stop her. She didn't deviate from her strong faith in God. She didn't give up. I now see her teaching, preaching and praying and ministering to the hurting people, letting them know there is nothing you can't do through prayer. My mom! a woman of prayer.

Best Girlfriends

Toya and Tasha have been best girlfriends, ever since they could remember. Toya and Tasha did everything together. Now they were approaching adulthood. They vowed to go to the same college. They recently received the news; they were both accepted at the same college.

Little did they know, they were about to go in two different directions. The day finally arrived, Tasha's and Toya's families were sad when the moving day came. They both told their families not to worry they have each other. Atlanta was a far cry from a small town from where they came from. They both were raised with morals, values and were family oriented.

Tasha and Toya arrived safely to their destination. Toya blurted out, "I'm so glad to be away from home." Now we can do whatever we want to do, party, go out, and meet new people. Hold on girlfriend, we are here to get our degrees," said Tasha.

Yea, I know, but we were always studying, we really never ventured out, never did anything crazy, we received a four year scholarship, hard work does pay off.

"Yeah!" Toya said. But, we need to let our hair down and meet some fine specimen. Specimen? Girl you better get your head out of the clouds, and remember what we are here for. All of that will come later, now missy let's get un-packed...call home and tell them we made it here safe.

Girl you are no fun. "Whatever," said Tasha. The girls were tired from the long drive and unpacking. It was time to get their schedules for class. Toya, wake up, Its about that time. No rest for the weary.

No rest indeed. It was a short walk from the dorm, Toya was checking out the scenery, there were men everywhere a lot to choose from. Girl, don't go hog wild. Remember what you have been taught, I know what I have been taught, but I'm going to have some fun. Girlfriend do whatever you want to do, I know it's by the grace of God, that I am here. Look at some of our friends, some didn't make it. Take Mary for instance, she at one time had the highest scores in our class, then, got involved with that no GOOD...

Watch your mouth Tasha, that guy was my friend. Toya! James had issues, when Mary found out he was two or three timing her, she just dropped out of sight, school and all.

Imagine letting a man, rather letting a boy ruin your future, because he was no man. I told you Tasha he was my friend, stop judging people all the time. I am not judging; I can see we are not going to agree on the subject of James Moore.

Okay, let's check on our classes, said Tasha. It was a long day Tasha went directly to the dorm to sleep. Toya decided to walk around the campus. She met a group of students, they invited her out, she accepted. Toya found herself hanging with this group of students often. Tasha and her, would often get into arguments concerning her choice of friends.

Toya told Tasha she was jealous because she didn't have friends. This group of students; were known for trouble. Toya kept missing classes. Tasha tried to talk to her about her behavior. It would always turn into an argument.

Tasha prayed often for Toya. Her constant prayer was for God to take care of her girlfriend. One day while Tasha was studying Toya came into the room, she was so high she was stumbling. Tasha asked her what was she, high on. I know you know better than to do drugs. How many times have we had this conversation? Remember the things drugs do to you. Please tell me you are not hooked, said Tasha. What if I am? It's none of your business. Toya we are friends, not just friends, we are best girlfriends, I care about you; I have been praying for you. "Pray for your self," said Toya. I'm tired of you, miss holier than thou. I have lived in your shadow for as long as I can remember. Everyone was always comparing me to you, I am tired of it. I had to do everything double just to keep up with you. Miss judgemental, do you think you are better than me? Asked Toya. I know it's the drugs talking, this is not you Toya. I may be high, but I know exactly what I am saying, I tried to be just like you. You should have tried to be like your self, not me.

My mom was always saying, Tasha did this, Tasha did that, you know I got tired of hearing your name. You don't mean that Toya. I do mean it. You are a royal pain, and always were, I wanted to go out and party and have fun, but little miss prissy wanted to go to church, choir rehearsals and youth bible study. I was forced to go because of you.

Now I have friends, my kind of friends. They are not your friends Toya, you are just someone to get high with. Your are just jealous, I'm the popular one now, not you. I had enough of this Toya, I'm moving my things to another dorm. Go ahead! What are you waiting for? I don't need you. I'll pray for you Toya. You do that girlfriend. Tasha left the dorm in tears. How could Toya say those awful things, they have been girlfriends forever. Did she really mean what she said? Toya and Tasha had never been apart like this before. Tasha left and moved into a room with another room- mate.

She was sad, but she knew she had better get to her home work, or she would be failing. After that, she didn't see much of Toya. She would only see her in between classes, on campus, hanging out with her friends. However, she never stopped praying for her friend Toya. It wasn't easy, because every time she would call home, she had to pretend everything was okay.

Days and months passed, classes weren't easy for Tasha, because she was worried about her friend Toya. Then she began to see her less often. Tasha had heard word around the campus that Toya was still hanging out with her new friends. Toya seldom attended her classes, her grades were falling. One day after her classes were over, Tasha could hear

Mr. Waller, one of Toya's professors , giving her a lecture about her failing grades and class absences. Toya and Tasha glanced at each other without speaking, only making eye contact. The first semester was hard and long, But Tasha managed to score A's on all her finals.

She thought about how it would be great to share with Toya again. She wanted things to go back to the way they were.. She laid on her bed reminiscing the good times her and Toya shared. She began to cry out to God for her friend.

God please take care of Toya, please help her out of this situation, lead her back onto the right path. Sometimes when you pray, you never know if God is going to answer your prayers right away, then Tasha fell into a deep sleep. Time passed, she didn't see Toya in her classes anymore, she had changed all her classes, so now she really didn't know what was going on in her life. Even though she was worried about her friend, Tasha knew she had to stay focus on her studies. She had dreamed of her and Toya becoming lawyers.

Then the phone rang; Tasha Randall? Yes this is she. This is Atlanta's General Hospital, yes? Your number was given to us as an emergency contact. Yes, what's wrong? Toya Alexander was brought in, she is unconcious from a drug over dose. Oh my God! I'll be right there. Tasha arrived at the emergency room, as quickly as she could, I'm Tasha Randall, she said as she approached the nurses station.

Come with me Ms. Randall, said the nurse. The doctors are waiting to speak with you, your friend is in critical condition, she is in a coma. We will know more as the time goes by. You better call her parents...and if you are a praying woman, this would be the time to do so. "You can go in the intensive care unit to see her," said the doctor. Tasha approached Toya, she looked so different. There were tubes everywhere, how did she get to this point? God did I leave her? Is this my fault? She kept asking herself a thousand and one questions.

How can I tell her parents? I should have told them what was going on with Toya a long time ago. Tasha sat by Toya's bed. She vowed to help her in anyway she could. She had to go to the lobby to call her parents. It was one of the hardest things to do. Toya was strung out on drugs and in a coma. She broke the news to Toya's parents. They said they would be on the first flight there.

Now Tasha had to call her mom. Mom! Yes Tasha, Muriel told me all about Toya. I'm sorry to hear the news...I'm coming with the Alexanders, for moral support. Tasha, don't beat yourself up about this situation. Mom! Tasha replied, she is my best girlfriend, I let her down. She said some harsh words to me, but I never stopped praying for her.

Every night I prayed for her. "Baby get off the phone and stay with Toya, we will talk when I get there," said Tasha's Mom. The night seems so long she stayed by Toya's bed holding her hand while she prayed for her. It's now morning Tasha had stayed by Toya's bedside all night. Tasha's mom and the

Alexanders arrived. Mrs Alexander began to cry. How is she? She is the same. Tasha why didn't you tell us? asked Mrs. Alexander. I don't know, said Tasha. I thought she would come to her senses, I thought it was just a phase she was going through. Tasha you and Toya are best girlfriends, you are like sisters, you were insuperable. She changed Mrs. Alexander, she is not the same.

That's enough Muriel, Mr. Alexander said. We need to focus on Toya. Baby wake up, Mrs. Alexander kept talking to Toya. Mom, I have to go to the school and inform them of what has happened. Also, I need to get my homework assignments. I'm never leaving you again Toya, said Tasha. Everyone took turns waiting in the hospital room. No change, the doctor's would come and go, with no news about Toya's condition.

A week went by. The head doctors spoke to the family. Mr. and Mrs. Alexander you need to be thinking seriously about moving your daughter to a rehabilitation facility. She is not responding. What are you saying Asked,

Mr. Alexander. Are you giving up on my daughter? No, but there's nothing else we can do for her.

Everyone began to cry. You need to make arrangements as soon as possible. Tasha walked out of the room with tears in her eyes. She walked down the hall to the chapel.

She kneeled down and began to pray, her prayer became intense. God, first I thank you for listening to me. I pray that Toya wakes up from the coma, restore her mind, remove the effects that the drugs has on her brain. Heal her, I pray for forgiveness for being judgmental towards her. God! Give us another chance, I promise I'll do a better job towards my best girlfriend. Then Tasha began to thank God for Toya. She quoted the scriptures in Isaiah 53:5 by his stripes Toya is healed, I believe your word Lord, and it is done by faith; in Jesus name, Amen!

As Toya was getting up from prayer; her mom calls to her, Tasha! Tasha! Toya opened her eyes. She is responding, the doctor's can't figure it out. Okay mom I'm on my way. As Tasha was leaving the Chapel, she threw her hands up and said, "Thank you Lord."

Tasha approached the bed where Toya laid, tears streaming down her face, she reached for Toya's hand. She held her hand and they both started crying. Don't try to talk, Tasha tells her. She motioned for the nurse to give her something to write on. She scribbled on the piece of paper as best as she could, she wrote "best girlfriends." The road was hard and long for Toya, she signed herself into a drug and rehabilitation facility, she took a year off from school. She changed her major to social work. She excelled in her school work.

Toya and Tasha went in different directions. Toya had some twist and turns, but she beat the odds because she had support from the people who loved her. Because of God's mercy Toya was able to obtain her God given talent. She received her degree in social work. She became a social counselor for drug abuse. She lectures all over the country at colleges telling her story to men and women because of what she had experienced. Tasha finished school and received her degree. She was made a partner at a well known law firm. The two girls maintain busy lives, but made time for each other, now older and wiser.

Toya married a doctor and had two children, a boy and a girl. Tasha married an entrepreneur, they have one son.

Toya and Tasha live down the street from each other; they all get together for holidays and special occasions. But after all they are still best girlfriends and if they want to have girl talk, they will just run down the street.

I'm a Big Girl Now

Two years old Justice wakes up, she turns over to the other side of the bed and noticed that all of her sisters were asleep. She tip toed out of bed where her sister Mariah, was sleeping "wake up" she said, "I'm hungry", no Mariah protested. "I'm sleeping", ask Makalya.

Mariah turned over and put the covers over her head. Justice was annoyed at Mariah. So she pushed her sister, Makalya, "wake up" she said I'm hungry, no Makalya said "I'm sleepy", ask Jessica. By now Justice is really upset with her two sisters.

Jessica rolled over and put the covers over her head. Well! Thought Justice, I'll fix my own breakfast. She didn't want to wake mom up, so she thought to herself, I'm a big girl now, and I can do it on my own. She ran to the kitchen. Now what can a big girl fix for her breakfast? She thought.

She opened the refrigerator, hmmm milk; she got the milk and put it on the floor. She thought what can I have with milk? Mom said it was a no no to touch the stove. She looked around, cereal! But it was on the counter top. She couldn't reach it. How can I reach it? she thought. I'm a big girl now. She went to the dinning room...she spotted a step stool.

Mom used this to get things down that's really high. She pushed the step stool into the kitchen where the cereal was, then she thought I might fall. But she said I'm a big girl now. She reached for the cereal on the countertop; it fell and spilled on the kitchen floor, oops!

Well, at least it's on the floor, thought Justice all over the floor, what a mess. But I am a big girl now. I'll clean it up when I fix my breakfast. She needed a bowl. This requires her to get on the step stool again. I'm a big girl now. I can do it. Step one, step two. She saw a bowl and a spoon on the counter top. Here we go...she carefully stepped up and then down again.

With a bowl and a spoon...She thought this

cereal needs sugar. But once again she had to step on the step stool again. Step one, step two, she only saw honey on the counter top, oh well, this will do. She carefully stepped down from the step stool. She sat in the middle of the kitchen floor. She poured the cereal, she missed the bowl. She wasn't being very successful. So she put her hands in the box, one scoop, two scoops, in the bowl. That should do it. She clapped her hands and said I am a big girl now. Now her other task, she had to pour her milk in the bowl

She missed the bowl. She thought there must be another way. She drank the milk out the carton and took some cereal, put it in her mouth yum, yum good. Oh, I have forgotten the honey, and she put the milk down, cereal in one hand and poured the honey in the other hand. Yum, yum good. Justice had a good time eating her breakfast. She ate until she was full. By now Jessica rolled over and discovered Justice was gone. Justice where are you. Jessica rolled out of bed. She began to look for Justice. She found Justice in the kitchen, milk, cereal and honey all over the floor, Justice! Jessica shouted. "I told you I was hungry", said Justice. Mama! Mama! Jessica shouted. What is it Jessica? I'm trying to sleep. Mama you have to come and take a look at the mess Justice made, said Jessica. "I'm a big girl now, Mama", said Justice.

Jessica and her mom began to laugh. Mom said are you big enough to clean this mess up Justice? Yes Mommy, because I'm a big girl now.

Listen To Your Heart

Introduction - Chicago Present Day

Brittany Moore was a typical sixteen year old. It was late autumn, she had been back at school for about three months now, and the pressures of returning for her sophomore year had began to dissipate. She was settling into her groove and was starting to think about important issues in a sophomore's life. These were going to the mall and meeting boys. Brittany and her mother Lesia had a very healthy relationship

There were only two of them so they shared everything. Brittany, began to share her interest in boys and the mall with her mother, Lesia. Lesia would roll her eyes when Brittany talked about boys and the mall. Her mother, Lesia would tell her she was never going to find the love of her life at the mall or at a party, Friday night after the football game. She would find him in the classroom, he would be somebody who would challenge her and spark her curiosity. Brittany rolled her eyes back at her mother and told her she did not know what it is like to be a teenager or to have fun.

Lesia was a widower. Her husband Bradley, Brittany's father, died when Brittany was very young. Brittany did not remember much about her father. She only remembered what her mother had told her. Lesia's memories of Bradley constantly stirred inside of her. Everyday she would recall her days in high school when they began life together.

High School – Chicago 1968

It was 1968, there were many changes going on in the world and these changes were having a direct effect on Lesia Johnson's life. She was a senior in high school. The enjoyment she found in the friday night football games and the weekend drive-in movies were starting to fade. She was starting to think about her future and she wanted to find somebody who had the same dreams she did. She wanted to find a kind and thoughtful boy who was smart and respected her. She wanted a boy who she could help grow up to be a man. He would be no ordinary man, but instead he would be a gentleman.

Lesia was very pretty so she had a lot of suitors in high school. She did not want a lot of suitors, just one that she could spend her life with. As she talked about the upcoming prom with her best friend Brianna along came Bradley Moore. Everybody in school including Brianna thought that Bradley was a geek. Brianna like most of the other girls liked the football and basketball players. They were the cool guys. Lesia liked the cool guys too, but her secret crush was on Bradley Moore. Brianna would ask who was that guy. She would say that it is Bradley Moore, my friend.

After Brianna and Lesia finished gossiping, Lesia reminded her that they had a test in the next class. Brianna did not want to think about a test right now. All Brianna was thinking about was the party on the weekend all

Brianna ever talked about were parties.
Brianna was the party queen. Lesia enjoyed
parties, but there was more to life than just
parties. Lesia often thought about the future.

High School in 1968 could be broken down into
four components. These were academics,
sports, extra-curricular, and the social life.
Everybody's priority on these four
components, were not the same, but one thing
was for certain, the prom was the pinnacle of
the social life. Everybody was talking about
the prom. Brianna had the prom already
planned out. Her boyfriend for two years,
Marcus, who also happened to be the star
running back, was taking her to the prom.
Lesia had not revealed who she was going to
the prom with and Brianna continued to pry.
Finally Lesia broke down and told Brianna she
would ask Bradley Moore. Brianna laughed and
said you have to be kidding. Lesia had been
avoiding Bradley forever.

Lesia waited for the perfect time to ask
Bradley. Bradley had approached Lesia several
times in the past, but she would always tell

him to get lost. Bradley would always provide
the same response when Lesia told him to get
lost. He would tell her to listen to her heart.
Lesia would get furious and tell Brad he knew
nothing about her heart, but he would
patiently say to just listen. As the days went
by Lesia thought about how she was going to
ask Bradley to the prom. Nobody thought that
she would actually ask Bradley. She would
often get very close, but then would not go
through with it. Lesia was very popular. What
if Bradley said no? What if he just laughed at
her? That would be a hugh blow to her ego and
cause a ripping effect on her social life
throughout the high school.

Lesia finally had her perfect moment to ask
Bradley to the prom. It was after school and
nobody was around. Lesia walked over to
Bradley, and she shyly asked him to the prom.
He smiled and said, "No, thank you."

This made Lesia furious. "What do you mean
no thank you?" Bradley repeated himself.
Suddenly, the varsity football team started
filing into the hall where Lesia and Bradley

stood. Bradley asked Lesia to repeat her question. Lesia was still furious from the initial rejection and shouted out, "would you like to go to the prom with me?" "Would you like to go to the prom with me?"

The entire football team heard her shouting. They all shook their head in disbelief. Aaron, the star quarterback, had asked Lesia to the prom two days before and she refused. He was the most shocked. Bradley told Lesia he would gladly attend the prom with her. Lesia gave Bradley her phone number and address. Lesia and Bradley separated. As Lesia began to get ready to go home, she asked herself, why did Bradley have to embarrass me in front of the whole football team? She concluded Bradley was paying her back for all the times he asked Lesia out and she denied him.

The day of the prom was approaching and everybody was thinking about it with great anticipation. Lesia was going through the daily routine of high school, and she was sitting at the lunch table with her best friend Brianna.

Brianna asked if she finally gave in to Aaron, the star quarterback, and decided to attend the prom with him. This would work out well for Brianna, her boyfriend Marcus was best friends with Aaron, the four of them could attend the prom together, it would be the best party ever. Lesia told Brianna that she was not attending the prom with Aaron, but would instead be attending it with her friend Bradley. "Bradley, are you crazy?" Brianna exclaimed.

This is going to be the best party ever. "How can you do this to me?" asked Brianna. Lesia told her this is not just about a party for me. This is about my future. Bradley Moore is my destiny.

The night of the prom finally arrived. Bradley and Lesia walked in together. Lesia's friends did not say it aloud, but they knew in their hearts that Bradley and Lesia really looked good together. There was something relaxed and natural about the way they interacted with one another.

The night of the prom was magical. Everybody who was somebody was at the prom, but for Lesia and Bradley it was just the two of them. Lesia felt her heart skip a beat as Bradley and her danced to the slow songs. As they intimately talked to one another, Bradley told Lesia about his dreams for the furture. These dreams included college, his own business, children, and Lesia. After four years of high school, Lesia finally found her future, it was Bradley Moore. Lesia and Bradley talked and danced throughout the entire night.

College - Chicago 1969-1973

Bradley was the valedictorian at Roosevelt High School in Chicago and because of this he received scholarship offers from around the country. Stanford, Yale and Harvard had offered him an opportunity to study at their schools, but Bradley chose to stay close to home and took a scholarship from the University of Chicago. While Bradley was talented in all subjects he had a knack for business and numbers, so he chose to major in Economics and Mathematics.

Bradley worked hard to obtain his Bachelor of Arts from the University of Chicago and after four hard years of work and study, he completed his degree. He had made many friends at the University including students and faculty. He would use the knowledge he obtained and the connections he made to complete his dream of starting his own business. Lesia stay with him through all of his hard work through school. He would ask her to share in his dream.

While Bradley studied at the University of Chicago, Lesia chose to continue her studies in Chicago as well. Lesia loved to take care of people and she was smart so she decided to pursue a career in the medical industry as a licensed practicing nurse (LPN). There was an LPN program at Loyola University which was very close to the University of Chicago. Lesia was not Catholic, but she liked the idea of attending a University that was founded by

Jesuits. There would be a sense of
Christianity infused into her course of study.

Lesia's LPN program was a three year course
of study. The tuition was low because Lesia
would live in the dormitory, study during the
day, and work nights at the university hospital
while she completed her program. Working at
night in the University hospital was part of
her LPN program and would help pay for her
costs. It was a three year program and Lesia
completed her degree a year before Bradley.
She stayed on at the University hospital
working in the emergency room and studying
for her board exam while Bradley completed
his BA at the University of Chicago.

Marriage

After completing his degree from the
University of Chicago, Bradley took a job as a
trader on the Chicago Board of Options
Exchange (CBOE). It was long hours, and an
entry level position, but Bradley really liked
economics and he was good with numbers so

he considered it to be a great challenge. He worked sixty hour weeks, and this created a strain on his relationship with Lesia, but it provided money for him to purchase an engagement ring and savings for a down payment on a house.

After a year out of school Bradley asked Lesia to marry him. They got married in a small ceremony attended by family and friends. Both Bradley and Lesia were practical. Instead of spending a large amount of money on a big ceremony they would use it to put a down payment on their first home. They knew they loved each other. They did not need a big ceremony to prove it.

While Bradley started his career at the CBOE Lesia moved from the hospital at the University of Loyola to the Cook County Medical Center in the heart of the city. She worked a standard forty hour week while Bradley continued to work his sixty hours at the CBOE. Lesia would finish her shift and return to the empty house and wait for Bradley to come home late at night. This routine of returning to an empty house and waiting started to irritate Lesia. Finally one Sunday morning while getting ready for church Lesia confronted Bradley about his long hours. She reminded him how he told her to listen to her heart when they first started dating. Now her heart was telling her that she needed to spend more time with Bradley. Bradley agreed they were not spending enough time together, and he would need to come up with a solution to resolve their problem. Together they would figure out a way to find the happiness they enjoyed when they were younger.

A new Career

At the University of Chicago Bradley had developed a strong friendship with a fellow student in the field of economics by the name of Jay Washington. Jay was also a talented high school student from Chicago who had an opportunity to study at an East Coast Ivy League school after high school, but instead decided to stay at home and pursue his degree at the University of Chicago. When Bradley started at the CBOE, Jay began a career at Merrill Lynch. Both men worked long hours, and were away from home an extended periods of time. After working for large organizations for a few years they decided they could maintain a better work and home balance by starting their own investment firm. While a new business was a lot of work they could complete some of their work in the small office they had purchased and some of the work from home. The two men would be partners, but Bradley would make the decisions on the most important issues.

Bradley and Jay began their new investment firm and Bradley did begin to spend more time at home. He would spend time at the office while Lesia was at the hospital and return home when Lesia did, in order to spend time with her. He would complete what work he could from home, this made Lesia happy. Her husband was once again spending more time with her, and he was listening to his heart. They would attend church together every Sunday.As time moved on however, and the business began to grow Bradley spent more and more time away from home. He needed to meet with clients at night and on the weekends. The interaction with clients could not be done from home.

Soon Bradley was not attending church on Sundays, but instead meeting with clients at the exclusive Chicago Athletic Club. This made Lesia sad, but she thought Bradley was working hard to support the family, and once the business was successful Bradley would have more time for her. While Bradley attended luncheons at the Chicago Athletic Club, Lesia continued to attend church on Sundays. She was praying and her heart was telling her that whatever happens, keep your covenant with God.

Bradley knew Lesia was sad that he was away for so long, and he was not attending church, he grew farther and farther away from the Lord...So he thought he could make it up to Lesia. On Sunday Bradley left his luncheon early in order to be at home before Lesia return from church. When Lesia returned home from church she had a sad look on her face. As she entered the door and saw Bradley, a smile came over her face. Bradley was waiting for her. Perhaps he was ready to give up Sunday luncheons, and he was ready to return to church. Perhaps he had started to listen to his heart. Bradley handed Lesia a black box. Inside was a diamond necklace and diamond earrings. Lesia's smile soon turned to rage. Bradley did not get it. His salvation was at stake he did not really know the lord. When he was going, he was just attending for her sake. That was the whole point of him coming to church, to really get to know the Lord; to give his heart to him. He was trading faith and love for work, money and diamonds.

A new Family

Work was a place that Lesia found a sense of purpose and serenity in her life. She had made a few good friends at the hospital, and helping patients through their difficult times was something in which she found great satisfaction. While Lesia found a sense of purpose and emotional pleasure at work, she was not feeling well physically. In the middle of a shift she would have to leave her patients and run as fast as she could to the bathroom. She thought that it was stress from her home life, but her friends knew otherwise. They insisted that she go down to the lab to get a pregnancy test.

Lesia wanted to start a family, but Bradley insisted that they wait until the business was successful. But how was Bradley defining successful? It could take a lifetime for the business to be successful? It was with the fear of Bradley's attitude toward pregnancy that Lesia went to the lab to get a pregnancy test. The test was positive. Lesia was pregnant.

As her shift ended a million things ran through her mind as to how she would tell Bradley the news. She returned home for the evening, and she fixed Bradley his favorite dinner. To her surprise Bradley returned home earlier than usual. They greeted each other with a kiss and Lesia asked Bradley how

his day had gone. Bradley responded that
Lesia did not want to know. Bradley returned
the question and asked Lesia how her day had
gone. She responded that she had a pleasant
surprise. She was pregnant and they should be
happy.

Bradley began to complain how he worked 12
hour shifts to make the business successful,
and he might not have much time to spend
with her and the baby. Lesia told him that she
would be caring for the baby, she is the one
that is pregnant, not him. Bradley continued to
argue with Lesia, so much that Lesia ran to
her room crying and slammed the door. The
dream of a perfect husband, home, and family
was turning into a nightmare.

Months passed and Lesia's stomach began to
grow. The nurses laughed and teased her
about how big she was getting. One day as
Lesia was joking with her fellow nurses and
doctors she told the staff she had an errand
to run, and she would be back shortly. She
thought it would be a good day to go to
Bradley's office. When Lesia arrived at

Bradley's office the secretary greeted her, and informed Lesia that Bradley was in a meeting. The secretary began gossiping about how excited Bradley was to have a child. He really wanted to have a son in which to pass the business down to. This was news to Lesia. At home Bradley was always complaining about the baby. Perhaps he was only expressing his fears about the responsibility and demands it would take to raise a child.

As Bradley came out of the meeting and escorted Lesia to his office, he apologized for his behavior over the last couple of months. Lesia accepted Bradley's apology and forgave him for his behavior. She had an understanding of the fear he was going through. She told him that she and the baby were healthy.

Nine months passed quickly and Lesia survived the morning sickness, the difficulty sleeping, the constant visits to the bathroom, and the swollen feet. She continued to work throughout the entire pregnancy. While at work Lesia's water broke. She was in the hospital and she was going to have the baby. She asked her friend and co-worker Christine to call Bradley and tell him the baby was on the way. Bradley was in an emergency meeting and he would rush to the hospital as soon as possible.

As Lesia was wheeled into the emergency room she began to pray. Please God, let Bradley be here to see the birth of his first child. Lesia was in deep prayer as the sound of the doctor's voice broke her concentration. One more push the doctor said. As Lesia delivered their first child, Bradley rushed into the delivery room to see the baby being born. The child was a girl.

The Business

Bradley Moore was overjoyed with the new born addition to his family. He had a new beautiful girl in his life. He thought to himself. Hopefully she will grow up to be like her mother. She will be kind and patient. She will have a determination to help others. As Bradley pondered the new joy in his life, his thoughts turned back to his business. He was expecting a boy who would take over the business when he got older. Now what was he going to do. Who would take over the business

Bradley expressed his concern to Lesia. Lesia's immediate response was why a woman can't take over his financial business when he decided to retire. Bradley agreed, of course a woman can run my business. Why didn't I think of that? he said to himself. Perhaps my wife is smarter than I think, thought Bradley. Bradley and Lesia decided to name their child, Brittany. Brittany was Lesia's grandmother's name. She had the courage to leave a small farm in Alabama, and to travel to Chicago in order to start a new life. The new addition to the family created many changes in Lesia's life. There were cries in the darkness to come and comfort the new baby. There were diaper changes throughout the entire day and the trips to the grocery store. New born Brittany seemed to never stop eating.

One thing that did not change was Bradley's

long hours at the office. Lesia kept insisting that Bradley needed more balance in his life. He needed to at least attend church every Sunday with her and Brittany. Bradley's church was the business.

It was everything in his life. It took priority over church, family, friends, and meals. It was what was going to provide for the family. The business is where Bradley spent his Sundays. The only Sunday he did not spend at the business was for Brittany's baptism. He did not even think about the business on the day of Brittany's baptism. There was hope. Missing church and meals made Lesia angry, but what really hurt was the loneliness.

Brittany provided great joy in Lesia's life, but she was just a baby. She couldn't provide the same joy that Bradley could. It would have been so great if Bradley and Lesia could share in the joy of raising Brittany together. However Bradley was always at the office. Finally when Bradley missed another dinner due to work, Lesia broke down and cried as Bradley walked through the door late at night.

Lesia whispered to Bradley, "Tomorrow is not promised to anybody."

Day After Day

Life went on in the Moores' household. Bradley continued his long hours at the office and Lesia continued her work at the hospital. While Bradley had changed throughout the years, Lesia held true to her principle of helping people.

In the morning Lesia would put Brittany on the school bus and then went on to work. She would then proceed to work at the hospital. She found comfort with her friends and patients at work. Some days she would witness patients completely recover from their illnesses, and some days she would watch as patients passed from one life to the next. Whoever the patient she did her best to provide for and comfort them. She tried to live the values that she read in her bible everyday.

One day Lesia had a funny feeling while on a break. She knew in her heart that something was wrong with Bradley. Lesia felt an urgency to get on her knees to pray for Bradley. Dear God, what am I feeling? After the prayer she called the office, no answer, she called his cellular phone no answer. Maybe he stopped over Jay's house maybe, she would feel foolish if nothing is wrong.

She did not know how serious it was, but something was wrong. She went over to the office, and rushed passed the security guard. She ran to the elevator and pressed the button. It seemed as though the elevator would never arrive. Her heart was doing flip flops. Finally the bell rang and Lesia proceeded up to Bradley's office.

Lesia turned the door knob to Bradley's office, but she couldn't open the door. Something was blocking it. She pushed harder, and she got the door open. Bradley was not conscience, but he was still breathing. She called 911 and the ambulance came immediately. Bradley was rushed to the hospital and Lesia rode along with him. She prayed the entire way.

Life Goes On

When the ambulance arrived at the hospital Bradley was taken directly to the intensive care unit. Lesia followed Bradley and the doctors with prayers in her head and the bible in her hand. Brianna, Lesia's high school friend, brought Brittany to the hospital, and the two waited for news in the family room.

Lesia, called her minister, other friends, and family. Everybody rushed down to the hospital to support her, as family and friends prayed for Bradley throughout the night, the doctor came into the family room with his diagnosis. Lesia started out by saying I want you to be honest with me doctor, I'm a nurse I read his chart. The doctor's began to say. Mr. Moore might not wake up, he is in a coma. He has a brain tumor, the brain is swelling and he has complications, if we take him into surgery he may die on the operating table. Lesia told the doctor's that Bradley would complain about headaches all the time, but never took time to go to the doctor.

Mrs. Moore the decision is up to you, do you want him to have the surgery or wait, time is critical? Lesia asked,"could you give me some time to make this decision?" She went to the hospital chapel; she began to ask God for directions.

God what do I do, either way he might die, Lesia began to cry. She heard in her mind (listen to your heart), she knew within herself that Bradley wouldn't want to be a vegetable or on a machine to keep him alive. The most important thing to Lesia was Bradley's soul. Lesia prayed, please God help Bradley, help, him to believe in you. She went back to his bedside. He looked so different, much older, the cares of life. Lesia began to talk to Bradley. She rubbed his face, his forehead, she prayed, she talked to him. Bradley wake up, she said it again and again. Then her voice began to rise Bradley Moore wake up! If God is going to take you, then you are going to go right. I want you in heaven with me. The head nurse heard her talking loudly, she ran into the room and said, "Mrs. Moore you are in the ICU, please lower your voice." Lesia didn't stop, father God this is your servant Lesia and this is a soul, please save this soul, so that he can be with you in heaven.

"Mrs. Moore if you don't stop I will have to ask you to leave," said the nurse. Please a little more quietly. Lesia began to whisper in Bradley's ear, you will wake up in Jesus name...I command death to leave you. You have to give your heart to God. Bradley give your heart to God. If you listen you will know it's the right thing to do. She held his hands, they were so warm, Lesia said, "Bradley Jesus loves you." Lesia felt movement, she felt Bradley fingers move. Bradley she said, "you can do it." Wake up! He is moving; his eyes are opening. Mrs. Moore the nurse replied, "comatose; people do that all the time." No he's really waking up. Bradley slowly opened his eyes. He tried to talk, get him some ice, yelled Lesia. Mrs. Moore I have to take his vital signs, said the nurse. Listen Lesia said, "I am a nurse I will check his vital signs, I'll take full responsibility." Bradley, Lesia said, I want you to listen to me, do you want to give God your heart. Don't try to talk, just nod your head. Bradley nodded his head,tears streaming down his face, Lesia was crying also. Bradley repeat after me with your heart and mind.

God I am a sinner I repent of all my sins, cleanse me from all unrighteousness, your word says if I confess with my mouth I shall be saved. God gave you that little saying Bradley. Listen to your heart, your heart is cleansed. Bradley was crying, do you feel differently Bradley. Bradley nodded his head. God changed you. Bradley squeezed Lesia hand, after a while he raised his hands to heaven, and a smile was; on Bradley's face. Lesia seen his peace, his countenance changed in a matter of moments...Lesia laid her face in Bradley's chest and cried and thank God for saving Bradley. He put his hands on Lesia's back. Bradley's hand gently fell to his side. Lesia knew he was gone, she cried and continued to lay on his chest. The nurse said, "Mrs. Moore, he is gone I am sorry for your lost." It is alright, "he is gone to heaven Lesia said."

All of Bradley's hard work had provided a future for his family. The business was bought for an enormous profit by Jay his best friend. A trust fund for Brittany was put in place and her mother was financially secured. This was done long ago by Bradley. Brittany decided that night, that she wanted to follow in the footsteps of her mother and pursue a career that would help people. She wanted to be a scholar and a teacher. Lesia stayed on her job until retirement.

Helping people was her first love. She started her own business, a mentoring program for young women. She did seminars on grief and making decisions for the future within balance. "Ma, Ma, can I go to the mall?" Lesia heard Brittany's voice and came back to reality. Lesia told Brittany she can go to the mall. She just had to be careful and be home on time for dinner. "Your father sacrificed too much to provide you with a better life" Lesia told Brittany. Brittany told her mother she would be home on time for dinner.

To Be Kind is Devine

Sometimes God put people in our lives just for us to be kind to them. They have suffered at the hands of other people and it caused them to be bitter. God can use your kindness to turn a person's heart around. God; will take you through a test, and you want to give up because the test is so hard it brings obstacles, pain, and humility. You ask yourself, why do I have to go through this? God is trying to prepare us for the task ahead, so that we can help someone else. Don't try to get out of the test. Go through with the task, you are going to learn something. You are going to gain something. So to be kind is devine.

My story is about a young Christian woman named Mary. Mary applied for an elderly home care aide position. She interviewed for the job and she was hired. She was to take care of a 90 year old woman. Mary was told all she had to do was give the woman her lunch and occasionally help her to the restroom. Seems easy right? Mary had no idea the difficult task that was before her. On her first day she arrived earlier than her designated time. She was introduced to the 90 year old woman. Mrs. L was the name they called her, she seemed to be a sweet old lady

Mary's first week was frustrating. Mrs. L was quite difficult, she snatched things from Mary. When Mary said good morning to Mrs. L. Mrs. L would say," what's so good about it?" Mary said it is a lovely day outside. She asked Mrs. L would she like to go outside. Mrs. L would mumble under her breath, but would never give Mary an answer.

Mary takes that for as a defiant no. Mrs. L would try to get her walker by herself, Mary would try to help her, Mrs. L would tell Mary she could do it herself. Mary would help her anyway. She helped Mrs. L to the restroom. Mary waited to help her back to her room, this particular day she asked Mary to wash her up Mary tried but couldn't do the job well enough for Mrs. L.
She snatched the towel from Mary and complained that Mary didn't know what she

was doing. Mrs. L was bitter, every chance she got she said something that wasn't nice. Mrs. L had many aides to come to take care of her but they didn't stay because of Mrs. L treatment of them.

Mrs. L didn't want anyone to take care of her but her daughter. However, her daughter had to work. It has been a strain on her daughter to have workers come in to take care of Mrs. L. Her daughter loved her and wanted the best care for her. She didn't want her mother in a nursing home. She thought the best things for Mrs. L was her own home. Mrs. L was in good condition despite her age of 90.

She had problems walking because of diabetes, but her mind was sharper than Mary's. Mrs. L would ask Mary to call her daughter at work, but her daughter gave strict orders to Mary not to call her, unless there was an emergency. So when Mary refuses to call Mrs. L's daughter she would sit in silence and she would be very annoyed with Mary. Mary would say to Mrs. L that she had to eat her lunch but Mrs. L refused. She would do this almost everyday, telling Mary she's not eating, but after a short time she would eat her lunch.

Mary finally had a little peace while Mrs. L was eating her lunch. Mary would pray silently in her mind, God she said I can't take this anymore. Mary never expressed how she felt openly. But in her heart she wanted to leave, but she couldn't she didn't have the freedom to go

She would hear something in the back of her mind. You are here to be kind to her. She would say, God! "nothing positive comes out of Mrs. L's mouth. The words would come right back to her again, you are here to be kind to her...She would think of ways to reach Mrs. L. She thought that if she is kind to Mrs. L why is she so difficult. However, Mary kept being kind to Mrs. L. Some mornings Mary would have to go into the other room and ask God for strength. One morning she had all she could take.

Mrs. L's daughter stayed home that day, she told Mary she needed to speak with her in another room. She started out by saying Mrs. L informed her that Mary had raised her voice at her. Mary was thinking that she should have, but she didn't she thought this was her way out of the situation.

She listened to Mrs. L's daughter, now it was her turn, she explained that everyday Mrs. L would go out her way to be rude to her, but she assured her daughter that she never raised her voice at her, Mary stated that she was raised to have respect for her elders and in no way she would do what Mrs. L say she had done.

Mrs. L's daughter looked at Mary and said she believed her, this wasn't the first time Mrs. L did this. She does this to get attention from her daughter and to get her to stay home, but her daughter asked Mary to please stay. Mary could have taken the easy way out, but she didn't she stayed on with Mrs. L. Mary continued to pray for God's directions to show her how to reach Mrs. L.

One morning as she was getting Mrs. L up, she began to sing old hymns. She went through out the day singing. To Mary's surprise Mrs. L asked, what was that song she was singing? A song she sometimes sings at church. Mrs. L got so quiet, while Mary sang. Mrs. L mind drifted somewhere else; you could see it in her eyes. She was in deep thought. Mary kept singing everyday and one day Mrs. L began to talk about the old days, reminiscing on her younger days. Mary listened to Mrs. L as she talked about how she was attending church and how she kept her faith alive. She had a desire to be in church but as she grew old and sick she wasn't able to attend anymore.

She seemed to be the happiest when she talked about church. She said people stop coming to visit her. She grew lonely all she had were the soaps on the TV, that's all she had to look forward to. Mrs. L and Mary would loose track of the time talking. Mary and Mrs. L grew very close. She looked forward to Mary coming everyday. They sang and shared stories together. After seeing Mrs. L's birthdays come and go, it was time for Mary to go another Chapter in her life. Mary had registered for school and it was time to leave Mrs. L and she had to break the news to her.

Mary prayed that it was something that she had done or said to Mrs. L not to revert to her ways of being bitter. Mary finally had to inform Mrs. L she was leaving. Mrs. L said to Mary that she was the only one that showed kindness to her. She asked Mary not to forget her, Mary promised she wouldn't. Mary promised Mrs. L she would visit.

After a while Mary did visit Mrs. L. Mary kept her promise. The aide who answered the door told Mary that Mrs. L was a sweet old lady. Mary smiled, because she then knew that Mrs. L had truly changed. She could hear Mrs. L say who is that at the door? The aide told her somebody named Mary. Tell her to come on back, when Mary saw Mrs. L eyes light up. Well, well, well, said Mrs. L, "you kept your promise." You came by to see an old lady. Mary said yes and she will continue to come. Mary and Mrs. L laughed and talked. When Mary got ready to leave she kissed Mrs. L on the forehead and left. God changed Mrs. L's heart. God put us in unfamiliar territories just as he did Mary. Sometimes we think we are not suppose to be here, and God is saying no, this is where I want you. God was saying to Mary just be kind to an old woman. God used Mary to change Mrs. L's heart of bitterness to love and care again. Mrs. L's daughter died Mrs. L was put in a nursing home. Mary found out where she was, she went to visit her.

When she saw Mary she chuckled. Mrs. L seems as though she was running the place. She was in a wheelchair, looking good. Mary didn't know if Mrs. L would remember her because it had been some time since she had seen her, she had to find out where Mrs. L was located.

Mrs. L did not forget who Mary was. Mary lost contact with Mrs. L when she moved from Chicago. She was 98 years old then. Nobody knew how long Mrs. L lived. Mary was instrumental in Mrs. L growth process, despite

her age. So to be kind is devine. You never
know when you are going to need it.

Fond Memories of Grandpa and Grandma

Opening

I was born in a small town in rural Alabama. My grandpa George was a share cropper farmer. Grandpa George married my Grandma Lula and they had thirteen children.

My mom Earnestine was the seventh child of Grandpa George and Grandma Lula or Ticket and Lula, as they affectionately called one another. All together there were ten girls and three boys. Mom grew up on the farm, spending time with Grandpa in the fields learning how to grow crops, pick cotton, and tend to the animals. Mom and Grandma's favorite place was the kitchen.

While Grandma could make a delicious meal from any leftovers around the kitchen her most prized dish were her biscuits. Grandma taught my mother how to make the most delicious biscuits and she passed on this skill to me, but I couldn't make them quite like her. While my mom loved to spend time with

Grandma and Grandpa a new love eventually came into her life. His name was Samuel Reeves, my father. They were married at an early age. Their dreams were going to be realized in the big cities of the north

Chicago

At the age of three my parents packed up all our belongings and set off for Chicago, leaving behind the only world that they had known. While I know my parents must have been both excited and terrified at this adventure. They wanted to provide a better life for me and my siblings soon to follow.

We settled in Chicago, my father found a job. Soon I had new brothers and sisters being born into the family. All these changes were an exciting time for me. However, when my father told us that we were packing up the car to return to Alabama for two weeks in the summer to visit. It was great joy

Back Home in Alabama

I missed my grandparents so much and the fond memories, I had as a small child. Their home was not a large structure, but there was always enough room for my parents and eight sibling.

What I remembered most, and what struck me most vividly, was when I opened the car door to run and hug my grandparents. I enjoyed seeing the love and affection they had for us and the love and affection they had for each other.

Chicago was where we lived now, but the farm in Alabama was my home for two weeks every summer. After embracing my grandparents, we proceeded into the house. We enjoyed a nice conversation about what we had been doing for the past year and then it was time for bed. It had been a long drive from Chicago, but now we were finally back on the farm. In the mornings, I would rise early before any of my brothers and sisters. I would watch my grandma pray. This was her time to reflect on her life, and ask God to help her through the day. I always admired my grandma for this practice. I think that it gave her great strength.

The Kitchen

After grandma determined she was ready to start her day, she moved on to make a fire in the fireplace. This would take a chill out of the air and spread heat throughout the house. After finishing with the fire place, grandma would go into the kitchen and make a fire in the wood stove to cook morning breakfast.

This one particular morning, she was going to make her famous biscuits. They were famous because everybody loved them. Nobody could make biscuits like Grandma Lula. While my grandma loved the kitchen, my grandpa found his peace in the outdoors. Through the kitchen window I heard my brothers playing outside with grandpa's goats. In grandpa's eyes this was a definite no, no. He explained to us a long time ago that we weren't allowed to play with his goats or any other animals. His animals were his prize possessions.

Grandpa was in the backyard, singing and cutting more wood for the wood stove. He wanted to make sure grandma didn't run out because they would use the wood for different things. Grandpa could spend all morning cutting wood, but there were other chores that needed to be completed during the day. One of the chores was retrieving water from the well.

The Peach Tree

On the way to the well Aunt Lue and I had to pass a little old house owned by a woman named Ms. Rosie. She had a big peach tree in her yard. She had warned us several times before not to pick peaches off her tree. As we walked by her house on the way to the well that day, she watched us. We didn't take any peaches that day, but it was very tempting

Later that week grandpa asked us to retrieve water again from the well. Again we passed by Ms. Rosie's home. This time the peaches were irresistible. We looked for Ms. Rosie and in not finding her we ran over to the tree to indulge in those peaches. We could not resist, Ms. Rosie like the days before had been watching us. She told grandpa about what we had done. When grandpa found us he gave us a long drawn out scolding. He went on for what seemed like hours about how it was wrong to take fruit that was not ours. I thought he would never stop. He didn't let us off the hook. He reminded us that what we did was wrong. I promised to never do it again, if only to keep grandpa from lecturing us.

It was now late in the afternoon...Grandma would let us go down the road to visit a really nice lady named Ms. Willie Mae. She had a fig tree in her yard. She would offer us some figs, but I always said no. It was the peaches that I craved. We spent half our days at Ms. Willie Mae home playing baseball with her nephew.

Dinner

As the evening grew near however, you could hear grandma calling us to come home. We would be excited because dinner was a special time. Grandma's home cooking was a special meal. The bantering between grandpa and grandma was always playful. It was if they had their own secret code when they talked to one another.

My grandparents would affectionately shout at each other. Grandpa would ask grandma, "Old woman is my food ready!" she would talk smart to him and call him old man.

She brought him his food as if he was the king of the castle. In which he were. You could see the love they had for each other, but they had their own way of showing it. They were so comical. After dinner we would continue our conversation on the porch. Talking until late in the night or until the mosquitoes decided it was time for us to go inside the house.

Stories in Alabama

You could hear grandpa in the early mornings he would always get up early to feed his animals: the cows, pigs, and chickens. Grandpa talked to his animals; in some way they seemed to understand him. His days were full and busy. He was a great story teller when he had time. He had us laughing; my father would say "is that true daddy?" He called grandpa daddy. I don't know if all grandpa stories were true, but they would be so vivid and funny, he made you feel like you were there when they happened.

We visited an older gentleman by the name of Mr. Roberts. He would tell us how our parents were when they were growing up in the south. How the crops were doing and how people were changing. He talked about the good old days, he would call them. We would always promise to go back and see him.

There were so many interesting people in Alabama. Ms. Lizzie was a storyteller too. Her stories were often stories about the town and the people, but enjoyable stories. She knew everyone around and how they were doing. The days and nights were hot in Alabama. However, it was just exciting being there, everyday was an adventure. Grandma had her day planned and this day it included us picking berries for berry pie. Grandma gave us buckets to pick the berries.

Our buckets would be full. Of course we had to sample the berries before we got home. Grandma had a garden with lots of vegetables which she grew herself. Some days we would be on the porch snapping beans laughing and talking. I would get in the swing on the porch, swinging back and forth. Talking with grandma, she had a lot of wisdom she was so easy to talk to.

In early mornings, the dew was so thick on the grass, it seemed like it rained the night before. The sky was so blue and beautiful, the sun was shining and not a cloud in the sky. Grandpa was moving around, despite his old age. He could move around as fast as we could. He would race with us and he would win.

This particular morning Grandpa got his mules and hitch them to the wagon, he said he was going to go haul some wood to bring back to the house. Of course we wanted to go with him. It was fun riding in the wagon. Grandpa made it looked so easy, but you had to keep the wagon straight on the road.

Grandpa would say to his mule, whoa mule, geddie up mule. They really obeyed him. We were going down the road. People would come out of their houses to speak to us. Grandpa had a story about everyone we came in contact with that day.

Some people would be walking, passing by and would say, going by now. I asked my grandpa why they didn't just go on by, instead of saying it. It was just their way of communication. I have an interesting family. My other grandmother, my father's mother, also lived in Alabama. We had to split our vacation stay at each of our grand parents houses. My aunt Lue and I would walk to grandma Pearlie's farm, it seemed to be such a

long walk. They also had a large family.
Grandma Pearlie was a very stern woman who
ran her house with an iron fist. Everyone had
chores there. My aunt Carrie was going about
her everyday chores and she asked me to help.

Well, I thought to myself I was on vacation at
grandma; Pearlie's house and I didn't have to
help aunt Carrie with her chores. Aunt Carrie
told grandma; Pearlie I didn't want to help her
with her chores; she called me into the
kitchen where she was. It seemed to be her
favorite place, she was always cooking. When
grandma; Pearlie called you, everyone knew
you were in trouble.

She really scolded me for not wanting to help
auntie Carrie. She explained to me if I
pitched in, the faster aunt Carrie and I could
go and play. Of course I didn't see it that way.
I was upset with aunt Carrie for telling
Grandma Pearlie I did not want to help. I was
upset with Grandma Pearlie for telling me to
help aunt Carrie. After all I was on vacation.

I told Grandma Pearlie I wasn't coming back to her house to play with aunt Carrie. They all laughed at me, but I was dead serious, if my parents would allow me to. Overall I had fun. There were chicken, horses, cows and pigs.

My father's brother had the chore to milk the cows, and get the laid eggs from the chickens roost. I even tried to milk a cow it felt really funny. Grandma Pearlie was also a good cook like my other Grandmother. But what I remember most was her cakes. She would put them in the cabinets to cool.

It was very tempting to touch them. Grandma had something that's called a churn. It made fresh butter. It was an interesting process to watch her make. They made everything, homemade in the south. Even homemade ice cream it was the best tasting ever Grandma Pearlie also had a garden full of things she grew, I remember picking okra, tomatoes and squash. Grandma Pearlie would cook fried green tomatoes, everyone liked them but me. It was always something I didn't like to eat. I went from place to place watching my aunt and uncles doing their chores. My aunt Lillie had the chore of feeding the dogs. The dogs were very well treated. The dogs were my Grandpa Boe T's hunting dogs. He was a laid back easy going man. The dogs were black and white, spotted hunting dogs. They could run really fast. Well anyway, while my aunt Lillie was getting the dogs food ready to feed them, the dogs got into a fight among themselves, they made her mad and she threw a huge bucket of water on them

I said to myself I could get Aunt Lillie in trouble but I decided it was our little secret. I went over to the pig pen to watch my uncles feed the pigs. They were very large in size, I could ride them if I wasn't scared. Now all the chores were done. My aunts Carrie and Lue were on the porch laughing and talking, mainly about boys. Aunt Lue was a little older than I, so I wasn't included in their little secret conversation. However they better not let Grandma hear them, when she comes around, you better be talking about school or something else.

Everyone said I have features like Grandma and also have her ways. I couldn't see it until I was older.

I enjoyed every moment I was there. It was time to take that long ride back to the city up north. I would always be in tears to leave my grandparents

The two weeks always went by in an instant. It was time to return to Chicago. I was never ready to go back home. While my sisters and brothers didn't enjoy themselves like I did; these were always the best two weeks of the year.

On the long ride back to the city up north I would play the two weeks back over and over in my head. Sometimes the memory could be as enjoyable as the actual experience. I learned so many things in Selma, Alabama. I learned to be grateful for what I have and enjoy the small things in life. I learned family is important because they carry history. I learned to never take life for granted. I am older now and I have spent many more years in the city than in the country, but nobody can take those fond memories of my grandparents away from me.

Angel's Journey

Angel was the apple of her Daddy's eye. They had a special relationship. Angel was the oldest of 8 children. Her mom and dad sacrificed a great deal for their children

They had dreams of them being successful, especially Angel. They thought for sure she was going to be a successful business woman the way she approached things, head on. Angel's parents raised their children with moral values, they grew up in a church setting. All Angel knew was church, in which she loved. Angel was outgoing and fun to be around. Angel had aunts that were older than her, of whom she hung with.

They were also involved in the church. This particular day, Angel went to visit her aunt, her aunt had a room-mate and her room mate's brother Jonathan came to visit his sister. Angel was introduced to him; a relationship was formed. Everyone seemed to be fond of this young man, the church members and her family members. The older generations would say he was a fine gentleman.

Although Jonathan was a little older than Angel, it didn't seem to be a problem with her mom and dad and the rest of the family. It was very surprising because age was always a problem before. Jonathan had a car, a job and all the necessary things her dad thought was necessary for a man to have.

One day Angels church was hosting a banquet, Angel invited Jonathan. Angel's dad teased her about it. Angel's dad kept saying look like snow to me Angel her dad stated. Jonathan might not pick you up Angel, I might have to take you, he teased her all day. To Angel's surprise that's exactly what happened .

Jonathan's car broke down and Angel's dad had to drop her off. Jonathan called and told her he will meet her at the banquet, and might be a little late, because he was getting his car serviced. Angel was so nervous, Jonathan finally arrived, but she couldn't eat her dinner in front of him.

That never happened before, Angel not being able to eating in front of other people. But at $35.00 per plate she knew sooner or later, she had better eat her dinner. An opportunity came, Jonathan excused himself from the table. Angel, ate all her food in a hurry. Angel's friends made fun of her all night. Through all the fast eating and talking, it was actually a good night. All her friends seemed to like Jonathan.

During the course of Angel's and Jonathan's relationship, things began to change. Angel began to feel she was being controlled and pressured. She knew she didn't want any part of this pressure. She never experienced this before. It was different she didn't feel free to be herself. She didn't share with anyone about Jonathan's behavior. Everyone thought he was her blessing. Everyone was already talking about them getting married

All they saw was a handsome and fine

gentleman. The relationship became strained; one day Jonathan announced to Angel he was taking a trip to his hometown. But before he left, he made Angel promised not to hang her with her friends while he was gone.

There always seems to be an argument between the two of them about her hanging out with her friends. Angel didn't know if this was because he was older or he wanted to control her. It didn't feel right but she stupidly agreed not to hang with her friends while Jonathan was gone. A week went by, no calls from Jonathan.

The next week Jonathan called, stated he was back in town, he asked if he could come over, they needed to talk. He came over with a big stuffed rabbit he started out by saying he had something to tell her. He began to say during the week he was gone, he ran into his ex-girlfriend.

He was with her the whole week while he was there. He then began to play the blame game. He stated that it was a mistake for him to

Love Is a Journey...Short Stories of Love

have been with his ex-girlfriend. Angel listened by now she felt stupid for staying in the house waiting on his call. He went on to make a statement that he was a man, and if Angel had done things differently, concerning their relationship, he would not have been with his ex-girlfriend. The arguments went back and forth. Angel's voice began to rise, she asked him to get out of her house and take the stuffed rabbit with him.

She was in a rage, she told Jonathan she wouldn't take the blame for the choices he had made. She began to say he did her a favor. She felt that he was controlling her life and putting pressure on her. Also he didn't want her to attend church. Angel's parents heard all the commotion and screaming she was doing. They came out of their room, Jonathan spoke and apologized to them for all the trouble and left. She began to tell them half of the story, but before she could finish, to her surprise, they spoke on Jonathan's behalf. They said Jonathan was honest with her, she was furious with them.

89

They wanted her to keep the relationship with Jonathan. What a long drawn out night. Nothing was accomplished, just disagreements between Angel and her parents. When the word had gotten out that Angel and Jonathan had broke off their relationship, everyone tried to give Angel advice. They were saying things like: everyone makes mistakes, and how she needed to forgive Jonathan. Well to Angel it was a whole week of mistakes. It seemed as though everyone was against the decision she made to not see Jonathan again. No one seemed to understand she was going through...she prayed about her decision.

However, he didn't stop coming over to her house or calling. Every time she realized he was at her home talking with her mom, she would leave. Time had past and Angel continued her life in church, being active and doing the things she loved to do. Her laughter and drive was back. However, Angel and Jonathan continued to be the talk of the town. It's taken Angel some time, but she had finally gotten over her relationship with

Jonathan. One day Angel was over her friend Charmaine's house.

Charmaine's cousin Joseph came in the front door, they were introduced, he had such a beautiful smile. As time went by they became friends. They were always having a debate about one thing or the other. In the middle of these debates Angel and Joseph fell in love. While being with Joseph, Angel didn't feel pressured or controlled, this relationship was different.

She could tell Joseph things she never could tell anyone. She could be herself with him. But Angel's parents and other family members didn't approve of Joseph. They thought Angel was on the rebound and they thought as time passed she would put this behind her. They thought it was a phase she was going through. Although years had passed. They all thought Angel still loved Jonathan.

He would call from time to time but nothing changed Angel's mind. She was in love with Joseph. As time passed Joseph asked Angel to marry him, she accepted. Everyone was so shocked, she began to plan the wedding. She wanted to have the wedding at her parent's house, but that didn't happen. Angel's dad felt Joseph didn't have all the things he wanted for his daughter.

He felt Angel wouldn't accomplish anything in life if she married Joseph. He made it clear he will never support her in her decision. In fact he stated he wasn't coming to the wedding if she married Joseph. The father and daughter relationship was in trouble. Joseph would often find Angel crying, he would re-assure her that her dad would come around because he loves her.

Time passed, the wedding was getting closer; she was withdrawn about the situation, this was supposed to be the happiest time of her life. The man she looked up to, her father. She felt she could tell him anything. Now the relationship had changed. How could this be? She prayed and felt it was going to be alright, some how. She was happy and sad. Happy because she was going to marry the man she loved. But it was sad because her father didn't approve of her getting married to Joseph.

The wedding day had finally come. She had gotten ready. She asked her mom if her father going to attend, her mom replied, she didn't know. He didn't tell her. She started to go back into her room to do some last minute touch ups, when she looked down the hall, her dad was already dressed. Although he didn't change his mind right away, he was there to support her.

He didn't say anything to her, but looked at her with love. She could see it as they looked at each other, the love of a father and daughter. She knew for sure he would have problems giving her away in marriage to any man as well as Joseph. Angel and Joseph were married this was one of the happiest days for her.

One day while riding the bus to work, Angel began to reflect on her relationship with

Jonathan it wasn't meant to be. She didn't hold grudges; she realized he wasn't supposed to be her mate. She thought of the many times she shared with Jonathan about Christ. She didn't think he was listening at the time. She told him how happy she was being a Christian and the peace she had.

Many years have passed. This particular Sunday morning at church, an invitation was made for anyone who wanted to receive Christ in their life and to Angel's surprise it was Jonathan who walked up front to receive Christ. Jonathan became active in church, as the years passed Jonathan seemed to be blossoming as a Christian.

Although they were in the same church it was a large assembly. Sooner or later she was bound to run into Jonathan. And it happened; Angel glanced at Jonathan while they were going out the church doors. They exchanged hellos and small talk and he asked how she has been.

Angel had her 1 year old daughter with her he

stated that Angel's daughter resembled her. He asked her if she needed a ride home, she hesitated, but he said it will be okay and that he didn't mind dropping her off. He was going her way to his sister's house. All these years had gone by, she felt his peace. She felt when he gave his life to Christ everything changed about him.

The air was cleared, they began to talk about the morning service and how the pastor preached a good sermon. He thanked her for sharing the Gospel with him long ago, and being the person she was then. Although, it has taken him a long time to make up his mind, he didn't forget the things she shared with him about Christ.

Life is so uncertain no one knows when our time is over on this earth. Jonathan's steps were ordered by God. Memories clouded Angel's mind. Suppose she had shared with Jonathan about a life changing experience. Many years later Jonathan was traveling home and he was killed instantly in a car accident. Angel attended the funeral. She thought in her mind. Jonathan changed when he gave his life to Christ. Angel was sad about Jonathan's death, but happy about his going to heaven. Funny, how life happens. Angel is still married to Joseph 34 yrs and 9 grandchildren later, still in love with each other. What a journey Angel has been on, and she still continues on.

A second chance

Somewhere along in life, we will be tested beyond what we see. You have to believe God and believe in his word. No matter who has given up and see no need to continue. Some may even tell you to give up there's no hope. But you keep holding on because God gives you a word in prayer.

This story is about a middle aged married woman. Who have two teenaged children and whose husband has left the home and the mother continues to raise them with moral values and Godly upbringing despite her husband's absence from the home.

Her name was Mona. Mona was a Godly woman. She married a man by the name of James. They were raising their children in a church setting. They were a happy family. As time grew in their life, James began to hang around his old friends from the old neighborhood.

James did not see anything wrong with not

going to church on a regular basis. Soon he wasn't going at all. Things began to change in the family. Mona and James' relationship grew cold. He began to stay out all times of the night. He began to miss work because he was always intoxicated from the night before, he couldn't get to work on time.

Before long, he was fired from his job. Mona continued raising the children and taught them to love their father despite of what he has become. She continues to pray for her family and the effects it had on their children. James would disappear from time to time. Mona never knew where he was. Mona had to work hard and long, sometimes overtime to make ends meet. Because there was only one income, but she continued in her faith. She prayed for her husband to be reconciled to God and the family. James disappeared all together. Mona would hear talk that James was using drugs.

Things were hard for Mona and her children. Mona had to explain to her children why their father wasn't home anymore. Despite what was happening to Mona in her personal life without James, she didn't stop being active. She didn't focus on her situations. She worked in the children's ministry at her church she was involved in her children's school activities, God blessed Mona on her job. She was promoted to a higher position which paid more money. Mona was able to go back to school and get a degree in social work. Mona was happy except for her husband's absence.

Mona made a vow to God that she will continue in praying until her family is reconciled. So many people told Mona, she can forget about James, he is never coming back, he was too far gone even for her children.

Mona didn't accept what was being said to her, so she prayed in silence. She always had a routine to pray at 6:00pm before her children got home. One day as she was praying, her son and daughter walked in on her praying.

Daddy doesn't care about us. He left us. It's time for all of us to forget about him. We are not waiting for anything are we? Anthony's temper was rising up. Momma, you are a good woman he said, you love the Lord. Find someone who loves you for you. God knows daddy is not worth it.

Mona was upset with her children she began to say, I am the one who makes that decision. Don't talk to me like that about your daddy. You are young. I know your daddy loves us. He got caught up. He told me he didn't think he was good enough for us. He said that before he left us, he said we would be better off without him.

Look at how the enemy pulled him away from us. It was a plan to divide us. Anything God ordained, the enemy wants to destroy. Daddy was right about that we don't need him around here, he is no good. I am the man of this house.

Stop it Anthony you don't know what he has been through. You don't know his heart. For a man to have no self esteem about himself his childhood was rough. You don't know half of the story. Stop judging. You must pray

Anthony that when you get older, you won't do the same things your daddy did. It's just like Jesus, he wants us, but we don't want him. What if he's embarrassed by us? He still loves us, he doesn't like the things we do, but he loves us. He didn't throw us away. That's what we have to do for your father.

Momma, hold on, someone's at the door. Who is it? Who is it? Anthony was getting irritated because no one answered. Finally Mona answered the door she was at a loss for words. Hello Mona, hello James. Can I come in he asked? Sure come in. Momma who is at the door? asked Anthony. It is your father. What? Speak of the devil. "Anthony stop it," said Mona.

I know you are angry after all these years. "That is an understatement," said Anthony. You are let see, about ten years, too late. Where have you been dad?

Keisha was crying. How could you dad? After all these years, let him talk, kids. No momma I needed him, how about the father and daughter dance? How about the times I cried myself to sleep thinking I did something wrong to send you away? I graduated dad, top in my class. I kept looking back to see if you were going to show up. Well dad what's up, I needed you.

I am going to college to play basketball. I needed to talk about choices for my life. But you were no where to be found, probably somewhere drunk. Alright Anthony that's enough, mom said. James was so overwhelmed about all the questions. "Answer them James" said Mona. Keisha he said, "I watched you from a distance." I saw your graduation. Keisha you were valedictorian of your class. Good speech. I was proud of you. Yet, sad knowing that I have done nothing to do with your successes.

And you Anthony, I was there, at everyone of your games. I thought you didn't need me. I thought I was an embarrassment to you and your momma. I kept saying to myself you deserve better. I was no good drunk and high on drugs. I, was a nobody I didn't feel loved by anyone, not even myself. I hated what I was, and what I have become. I came to terms with myself and decided to get into a rehab for drug and alcohol abuse.

I continued and enrolled in school and graduated with honors. My degree is in counseling. But the most important thing was, I went to church while I was away and gave my life to Christ. I am a new person.

I strayed away from God and got mixed up with the wrong crowd. I know you were praying for me Mona. No one cared if I lived or died. I am glad God put me on your heart. I know I hurt you and the kids. I asked God for a second chance. I would pray every night about our family being reconciled.

I want my family back. I know it is not going to be easy. Dad! You think you can come back after all these years and expect us to just jump in your arms. It is not that simple.

Those years are lost, we are not kids anymore.

Keisha I know it is not going to be easy, if you give me a chance I am praying reconciliation. God also called me into the ministry and I am using what God has given to me to help other people like me.

I witness to people and tell them how God is a forgiving God and he is the God of second chance. I have experienced it for myself.

Mona could we have a word of prayer for God's directions. Wait James, I have something to say also. James I have been waiting and praying for this day, even when everyone said it was hopeless. I kept my faith in God and continued to pray. Prayer is powerful. James it wasn't your entire fault what happened. See when you left I began to seek God as I never before. I was so religious, I didn't have time for you. I had some issues in my life but couldn't see it.

I was so judgmental, but through prayer and counseling and an in-depth look at myself I am too a new person. Not only have I forgiven you, I have forgiven myself as well. I promised

God if he gave me another chance I will do it right. We can learn from each other. We will take it one day at a time.

I heard what the both of you are saying, but what about the pain and hurt you put mom, Keisha and I through? Are we suppose to allow you to come here and disrupt our family.

Anthony, I know it will take some time, could you forgive me for hurting you, for not being here when you needed me. Son I love you. I am willing to do whatever it takes, no matter how long it takes. I am not giving up on us. Jesus is our perfect example on forgiveness. He loves us unconditionally. I am willing to wait until you are ready, but I am not giving up on us son.

Dad, Anthony and I prayed so many times for you to come back, but it seems our prayers were in vain. I know God has a plan and a purpose for our lives. I don't believe this is one of the plans.

Dad the enemy had turned my anger into
bitterness. I did some things I should not
have done. But God turned me around I was
numb. Dad ,since God forgave me, then I know
I can forgive you, but it is going to be a
process, said Keisha. "you can go ahead and
forgive him if you want to, I don't need him, I
got a scholarship to play basketball, I got this
far without him." Anthony walks out the door.
"Anthony come back," did you hear me? Said
Mona. Let him go Mona, he needs time, said
James.

Let's go before the Lord in prayer, the enemy
don't want this family together because we
are going to win souls for the kingdom, the
enemy has stolen from us long enough. Mona,
Keisha and James kneeled in prayer, for
Anthony, and the family to be restored,
James knew it wasn't going to be easy.
Anthony was walking down the street seeing
what he can get into. He ran into an old friend.

Chuck my man what's up. Anthony what's going
on, same ole, same ole. Man, I have not seen
you for awhile. What's up? How are your mom

and dad doing? Remember your dad use to take us fishing, man you have a good dad, I use to wish he was my dad. I have a no good for nothing father. Man, I thought you knew. Knew what? Don't you read the papers, my mom and dad were both killed in a car accident? I would give anything to talk to my dad right now. Man don't take it lightly to have a dad, but Chuck you don't know my dad. He is been gone for 10 years, he shows up now and wants us to jump through hoops. He says he is changed and gave his life to Christ and he wants his family back.

Anthony when I lost my parents I was angry at the world. It didn't seem fair. My parents were good to me I have taken them for granted. They taught me what was right I didn't want to listen.

God called them home to be with him. What you know about Christ? You didn't listen when we were in Sunday school? I remembered everything I was taught but I didn't act on it until my parents died. I found myself doing things I never done, my moral values had changed. I stopped going to church altogether. I found out I was just a church goer, but didn't have a relationship with God, and I was only going because I was forced to go. But one Sunday I went to church still drunk from the night before, feeling sorry for myself. I could hear the preacher saying come unto me those who are heavy laden, man my burden was heavy. I began to cry and I gave my hurts, my pain and unforgiveness to God.

I was angry because God had taken my parents. I began to remember all the things my mom had taught me about forgiveness. I could hear her while I was at the altar, God loves you.

Man, I lost it. But really I found it. I found the love of God. Now here I am, being a witness for the Lord.

Anthony if your father wants a second chance then you should try. Ask God to help you. See, I can't talk to my father anymore, but you can. Life is so short; Don't waste it on bitterness and unforgiveness. Ask God to help you forgive your father. Anthony seek a closer walk with the heavenly father, don't be a church goer, but have a relationship with God.

Chuck you surprise me, you keep that up you will be a youth pastor, you are absolutely right. That is what I am. Thanks man I know this wasn't by accident that we met.

It was divine intervention. I will see you in church. Think about it. I will be there. Mom has been on me to go to church, but I didn't see the need, I was raised in church. I grew apart from it.

Man listen, God has a purpose for you in life, your mom is a prayer intercessor. She has always prayed for me and everyone else. Her request would always be to pray for her family to be reconciled and God has answered the prayer.

I guess you are right Chuck, but it won't happen over night. I am going home to talk to my parents. Man you do that, I am praying for you. We need another good man at church.

Mona and James were in the living room talking when Anthony walked in; Mom I am sorry I had you worried. I had a lot on my mind. Dad can we try, one step at a time. Prayer does work. I know it is going to be a process but I am willing to try. I do need you in my life. I am going back to church, I will start from there. I ran into Chuck from church. We had a long talk.

It is okay son, one day at a time. God has granted us a second chance. I can't make up for lost time but we can go from where we are.

Keisha comes from the back room Anthony I am glad you came back. Let's pray Mona said. James do us the honor and lead this family in prayer. You are still head of this family.

How We Met

It was almost as if it was yesterday. As I remembered it was about 35 years plus, on the south side of Chicago Illinois, on a crisp sunny afternoon. I had five brothers who I played with most of the times. I was called a Tom boy because I could play ball just like my brothers. I thought I was good until this Mr. Smiley came into my life, and caused havoc about me playing ball with boys.

I was playing football with my brothers. I noticed some one I never seen before on our block, at 85th and May. He had such a beautiful smile

I asked around, no one knew him. One day I went to pick up my friend Sharon for school, it was him, the guy who was watching me play football. He came to the door, my friend introduced us, we exchanged hellos. I thought to myself so this is Mr. Smiley.

I really wasn't ready to be in a relationship so I thought, however I continued to pick my friend Sharon up for school just to see this Mr. Smiley. I made sure I looked my best, but all he would say was hellos and good-byes and smile. Whenever I see him it seems to be a game he was playing so I played along with him.

As time went by, my brothers and I and the neighbors kids were playing softball in the neighborhood field, I was up to bat. There he was again watching me and smiling. I wanted to impress him; so I hit the ball far away, a home run. He shouted from the outfield, girls can't play ball or don't need to play ball. So I challenged him, he accepted, he would hit the ball far as he could and I will hit as far as he did. This went on for a while between he and I. Finally we stopped. No one won.

Later on that evening he came over to our house pretending to see my brother. I didn't know he knew my brother. He spent all evening talking with me, it seemed like hours. I felt as if I had known him for years. I felt I could tell him anything. I felt so free, I could be myself with him. He wasn't like the other guys I knew. We had so much fun, he made me laugh. I found myself wanting to be with him all the time.

We were very competitive. We found ourselves always debating about one thing or another. As times past I knew I loved him, I could feel it and see that smile he always gives me. I met the rest of his family and fell in love with them also they made me feel welcomed. This was truly ordained, it has been 35 years plus and my husband still has that smile until this day.

The feeling was mutual when he told me he loved me, then he played this song for me, we called it our song. "I stand accused of loving you too much," by Isaac Hayes. It has been a journey, it wasn't easy, we had some ups and downs, some trials and tribulation. Through it all we celebrated 35 years of marriage as Mr. and Mrs. Ronald J. Dyer Sr. To God be the Glory.

I Remember

Although Shirlene was my sister, I felt like a mother to her. I remember the many, many obstacles Shirlene faced in her life searching for her son, Ladel. Being hospitalized so many times, sometimes she didn't say a word, she must have been miles away in her mind. I also remembered the day she received her greatest joy. I was blessed to be a part of it.

Shirlene had been sick most of her life, her son Ladel, was taken from her when he was at an early age. He was twenty something when he finally met his mother. It grieved me so, that I began to pray and cry out to the Lord and I asked the Intercessor's to pray. My prayer was, not to let Shirlene leave this world without her knowing who her son was.

I began to search for him. He was stationed overseas in the army when I finally found him. The Lord began to deal with him, also about finding his mother. Prayer is a powerful thing.

God began to move. He was given my mom's telephone number, he called, and my mother was so surprised to hear his voice. She gave him the phone number where his mom was. He told my mom that he would call his mother from over sea's on Christmas day

I called the nursing home to inform them that Shirlene will be receiving an overseas phone call on Christmas morning. I asked them to have Shirlene in the front to receive her phone call. They said ok, but some how I didn't believe they would give her that phone call, if I wasn't there.

I drove over the speed limit to the nursing home, to make sure I was on time for the call. As I was coming in the door of the nursing home; the staff saw me coming, but didn't have Shirlene at the front, to receive her phone call. When Shirlene saw me, she asked what was wrong? I said nothing. I told her that I had a Christmas present for her. I pushed her in her wheel chair to the front desk. At that time the phone rang, they said

it's an overseas call for Shirlene, she picked
up the phone to answer it.

I heard the words mommy you are beautiful;
from the other end, Ladel must have seen her
pictures. She hollered and screamed, his name
so many times, what a wonderful Christmas
present, just the look on her face made up for
all the things she has ever been through, I
believed, to her, it was all worth it.

I remembered the reunion we planned for her
to finally see her son Ladel, for the first time
in over twenty years. Tears of joy flowed. I
cried and thank God for answering our
prayers. It was amazing, her dream had finally
come true. Some time ago, I was talking to
her and she said to me Chris, I have a
daughter in-law. Shirlene didn't think these
things were possible for her to have. I
appreciate God for allowing her to be happy
and to live so her son could be part of her life,
even if it was just for a short time, but to her
it was like a life time.

Shirlene Renee Reeves died in her sleep on

November 17th 2008 from complications caused by diabetes; at the early age of fourty-eight. She was on a journey and she finished it. Shirlene lived a short complicated life, a life filled with pain, disappointment, and heartache. However, by God answering her prayers, He made her life complete.

LaVergne, TN USA
11 March 2010
175647LV00002B/2/P